Dinosaurs

AND OTHER PREHISTORIC LIFE

POSTER BOOK

Editor Becca Arlington
Project Art Editor Kit Lane
Senior Designer Ann Cannings
Jacket Coordinator Elin Woosnam
Senior Acquisitions Editor James Mitchem
Managing Art Editor Elle Ward
Production Editor Dragana Puvacic
Production Controller Magdalena Bojko
Project Picture Researcher Rituraj Singh
Art Director Mabel Chan

First published in Great Britain in 2025 by
Dorling Kindersley Limited
DK, 20 Vauxhall Bridge Road,
London, SW1V 2SA

The authorised representative in the EEA is
Dorling Kindersley Verlag GmbH. Arnulfstr. 124,
80636 Munich, Germany

Material used in this book was previously published in:
An Anthology of Dinosaurs and Other Prehistoric Life
(2021)

A CIP catalogue record for this book
is available from the British Library.
ISBN: 978-0-2417-3107-9

Printed and bound in China

www.dk.com

This book was made with Forest
Stewardship Council™ certified
paper – one small step in DK's
commitment to a sustainable future.
For more information go to
www.dk.com/our-green-pledge

DK would like to thank the following for their contributions to the original
An Anthology of Dinosaurs and Other Prehistoric Life: Professor Anusuya
Chinsamy-Turan for the text; and Angela Rizza and Daniel Long for the illustrations.
Thanks also to Vagisha Pushp for picture research support on this book.

Poster list

- Dickinsonia
- Australaster
- Archaeopteris
- Dunkleosteus
- Tiktaalik
- Meganeura
- Dimetrodon
- Seymouria
- Helicoprion
- Araucarioxylon
- Stegosaurus
- Diplodocus
- Archaeopteryx
- Psittacosaurus
- Confuciusornis
- Sinosauropteryx
- Muttaburrasaurus
- Maiasaura
- Parasaurolophus
- Archelon
- Plioplatecarpus
- Styracosaurus
- Triceratops
- Tyrannosaurus
- Amber
- Smilodon
- Woolly mammoth
- Dire wolf
- Florissantia
- Megalodon
- Velociraptor

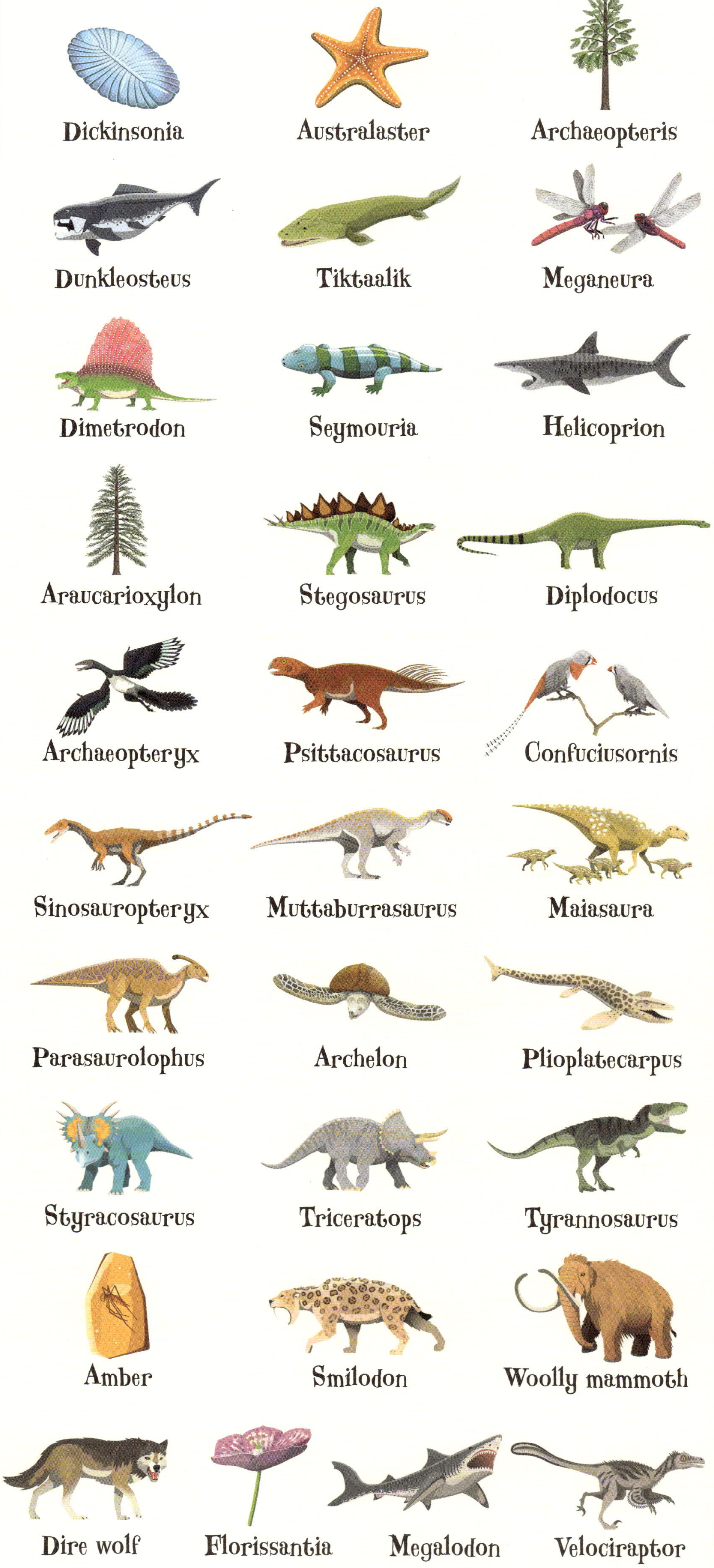

Dickinsonia

This creature lived around 567 million years ago and is one of the world's oldest known animals. Curiously, no mouth or gut can be identified in Dickinsonia.

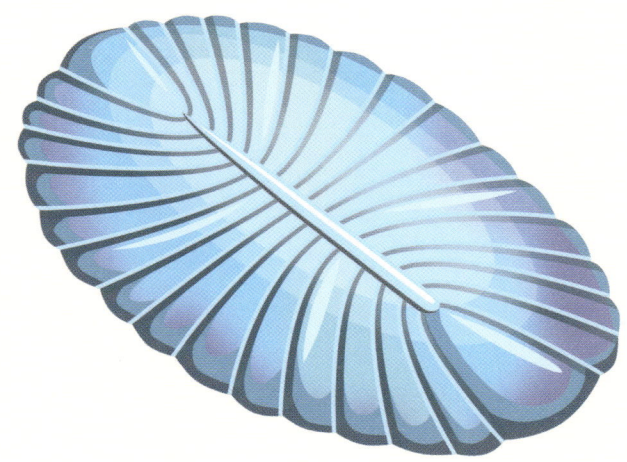

Pronunciation: Dih-kin-soh-nee-a
Period: Precambrian
Location: Asia, Europe, Oceania

Australaster

Despite being around 430 million years old, this ancient starfish looks just like a starfish today. Its name means "southern star".

Pronunciation: O-stral-ast-er

Period: Silurian

Location: Oceania

Archaeopteris

This was one of the first trees to grow on Earth, and it formed forests around the world. It had a surprising mix of conifer and fern features.

Pronunciation: Ar-kee-op-teh-riss
Period: Devonian to Carboniferous
Location: Worldwide

Dunkleosteus

This armoured fish had a bite force similar to that of Tyrannosaurus. Though toothless, its massive jaws ended in a razor-sharp beak made of bone.

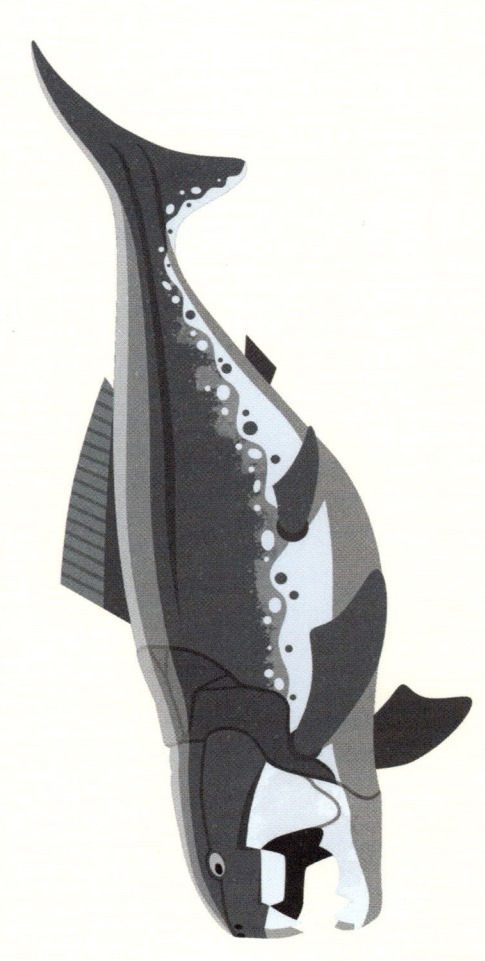

Pronunciation: Dun-kel-oss-tee-uss
Period: Devonian
Location: Worldwide

Tiktaalik

This animal's mixture of fish and tetrapod features shows how land animals evolved from aquatic animals around 375 million years ago.

Pronunciation: Tik-tah-lik

Period: Devonian

Location: North America

Meganeura

This insect was a type of griffinfly, the largest flying insects that have ever lived. Meganeura was even big enough to snatch up small lizards!

Pronunciation: Meh-ga-nyoo-ra
Period: Carboniferous
Location: Europe

Dimetrodon

Although this sail-backed predator looked a bit like a dinosaur, Dimetrodon was more closely related to mammals than reptiles.

Pronunciation: Dai-met-roh-don

Period: Permian

Location: Europe, North America

Seymouria

290-million-year-old Seymouria is thought to be a link between amphibians and early reptiles. It had many pointed teeth — even in the roof of its mouth.

Pronunciation: See-mor-ee-a
Period: Permian
Location: Europe, North America

Helicoprion

This bizarre fish looked a bit like a shark with a circular saw in its mouth. For over 100 years, no one knew where its tooth whorl was positioned.

Pronunciation: He-lik-oh-prai-on
Period: Permian
Location: Worldwide

Araucarioxylon

Today, this tree's fossilized trunks are petrified, which means "turned to stone". Petrification can happen when a tree dies and is buried by volcanic ash.

Pronunciation: A-raow-ka-ree-oh-zai-lon
Period: Triassic
Location: North America

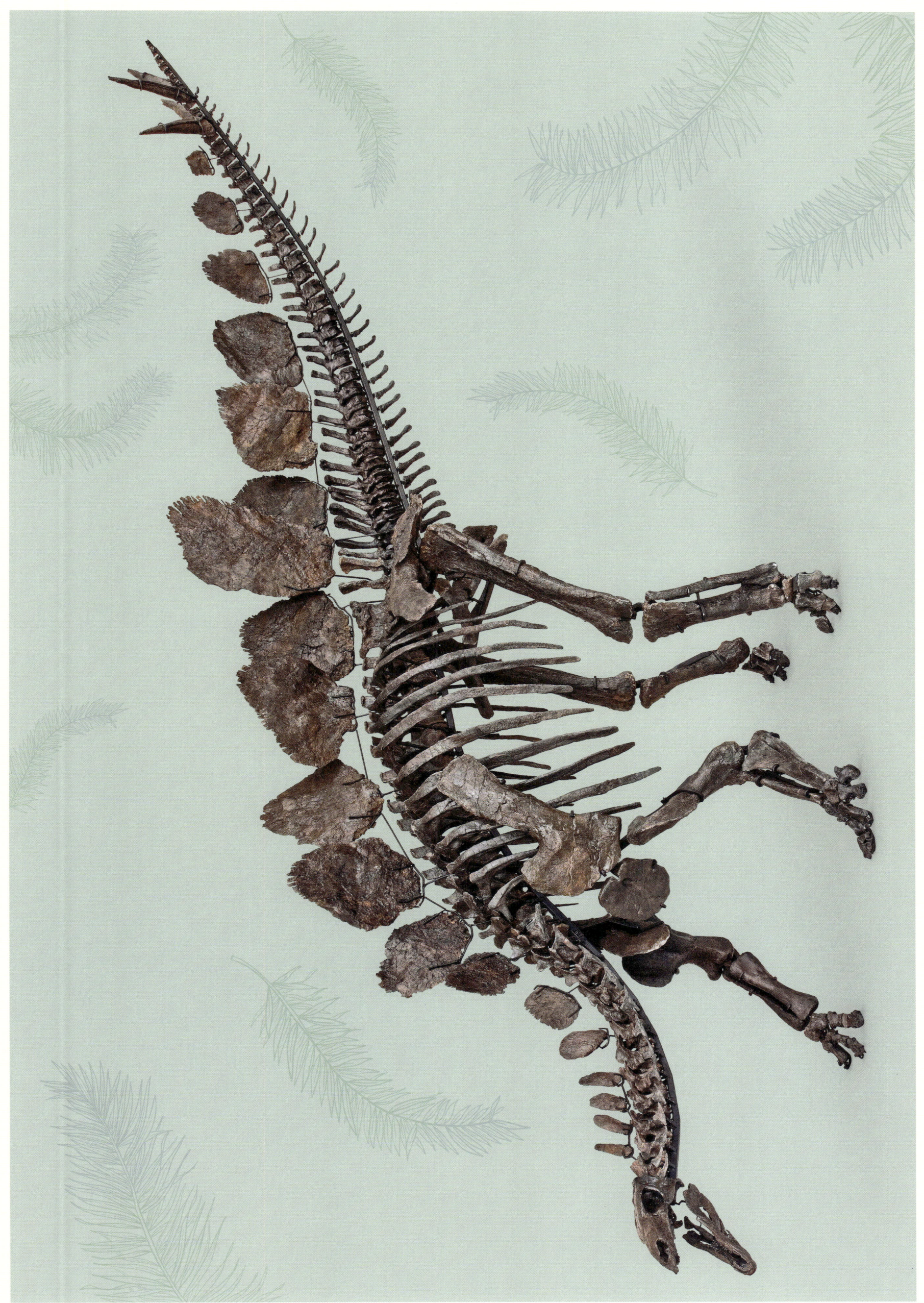

Stegosaurus

This was a dinosaur built for defence. It had up to 22 bony plates along its back, and four pointy spikes at the end of its tail.

Pronunciation: Steh-go-sor-uss

Period: Jurassic

Location: Europe, North America

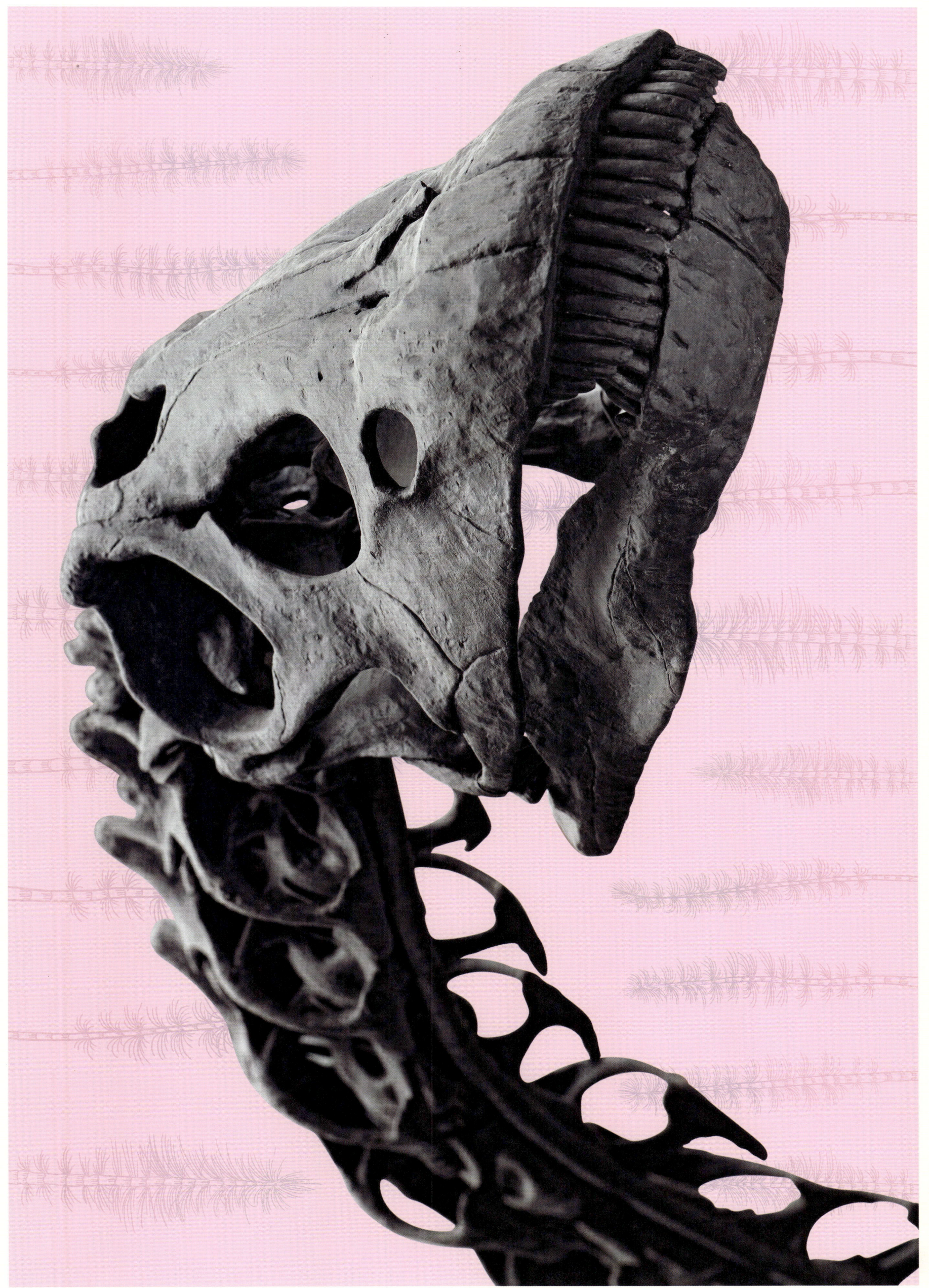

Diplodocus

At 26 m (85 ft) long, this sauropod was one of the longest animals to ever live – about as long as an average blue whale. Its whip-like tail contained about 80 bones.

Pronunciation: Dip-lod-oh-kuss
Period: Jurassic
Location: North America

Archaeopteryx

This was the first dinosaur with feathers to be discovered. It proved that birds are dinosaurs, and that dinosaurs live on today as birds!

Pronunciation: Ar-kee-op-teh-riks
Period: Jurassic
Location: Europe

Psittacosaurus

This dinosaur's name means "parrot lizard" due to the shape of its beak. Although it had no frill, it was an early relative of dinosaurs such as Triceratops.

Pronunciation: Si-ta-koh-sor-uss
Period: Cretaceous
Location: Asia

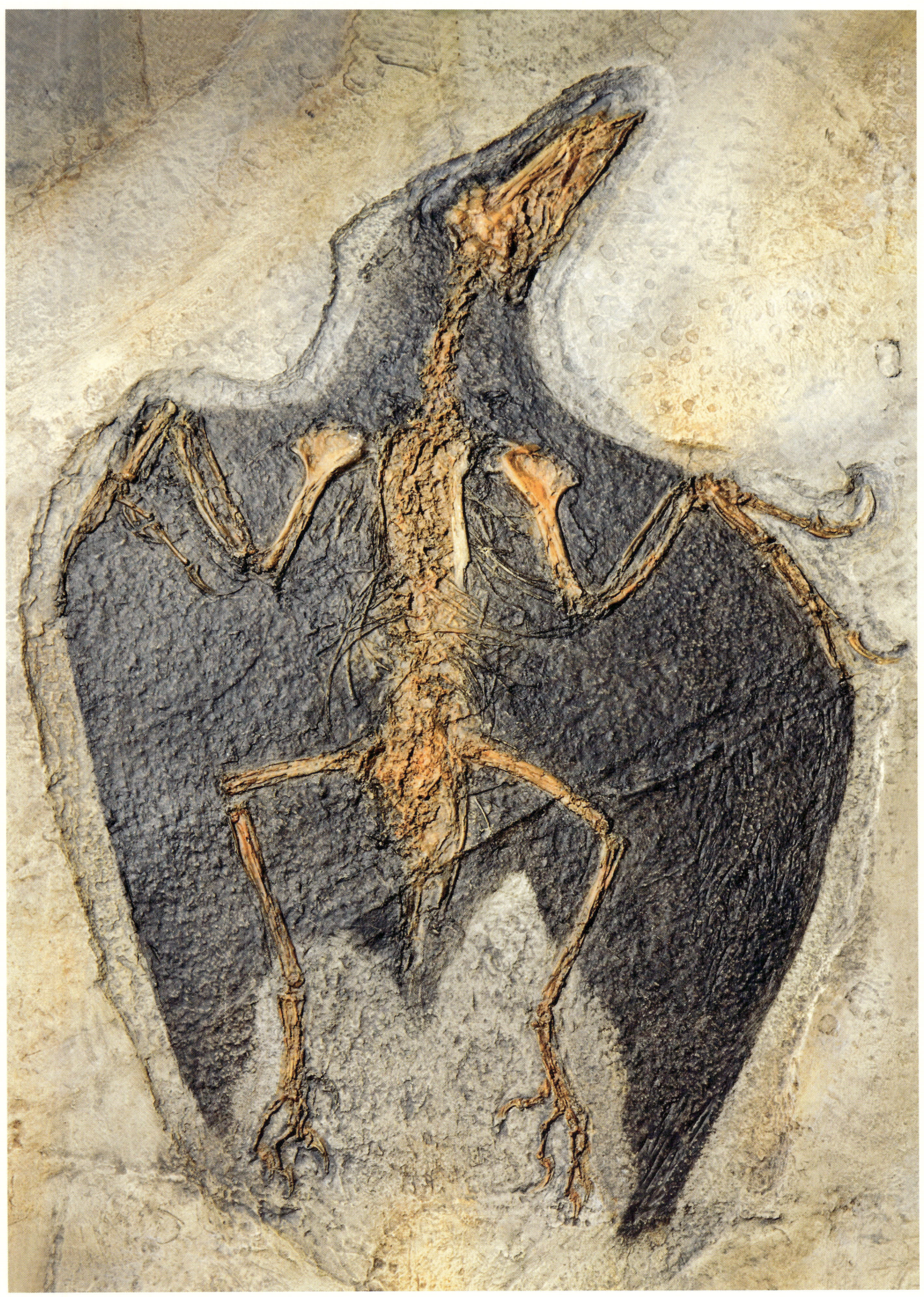

Confuciusornis

This was the first bird discovered with a toothless beak. It is suggested that male and female Confuciusornis looked different, like many birds today.

Pronunciation: Kon-fyoo-shuss-or-niss
Period: Cretaceous
Location: Asia

Sinosauropteryx

This was the first dinosaur without wings discovered to have feathers. Special structures found inside the feathers tell scientists all about its colour.

Pronunciation: Sai-noh-sor-op-teh-riks
Period: Cretaceous
Location: Asia

Muttaburrasaurus

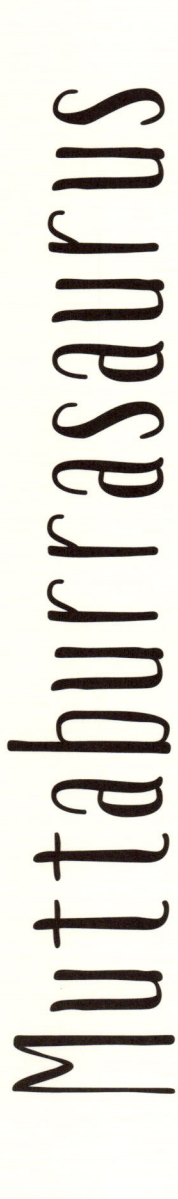

This dinosaur's most unusual feature was the bony lump on its snout. It is thought that it was attached to an inflatable sac that it could blow air into, perhaps to make sounds and show off.

Pronunciation: Muh-ta-buh-ra-sor-uss
Period: Cretaceous
Location: Oceania

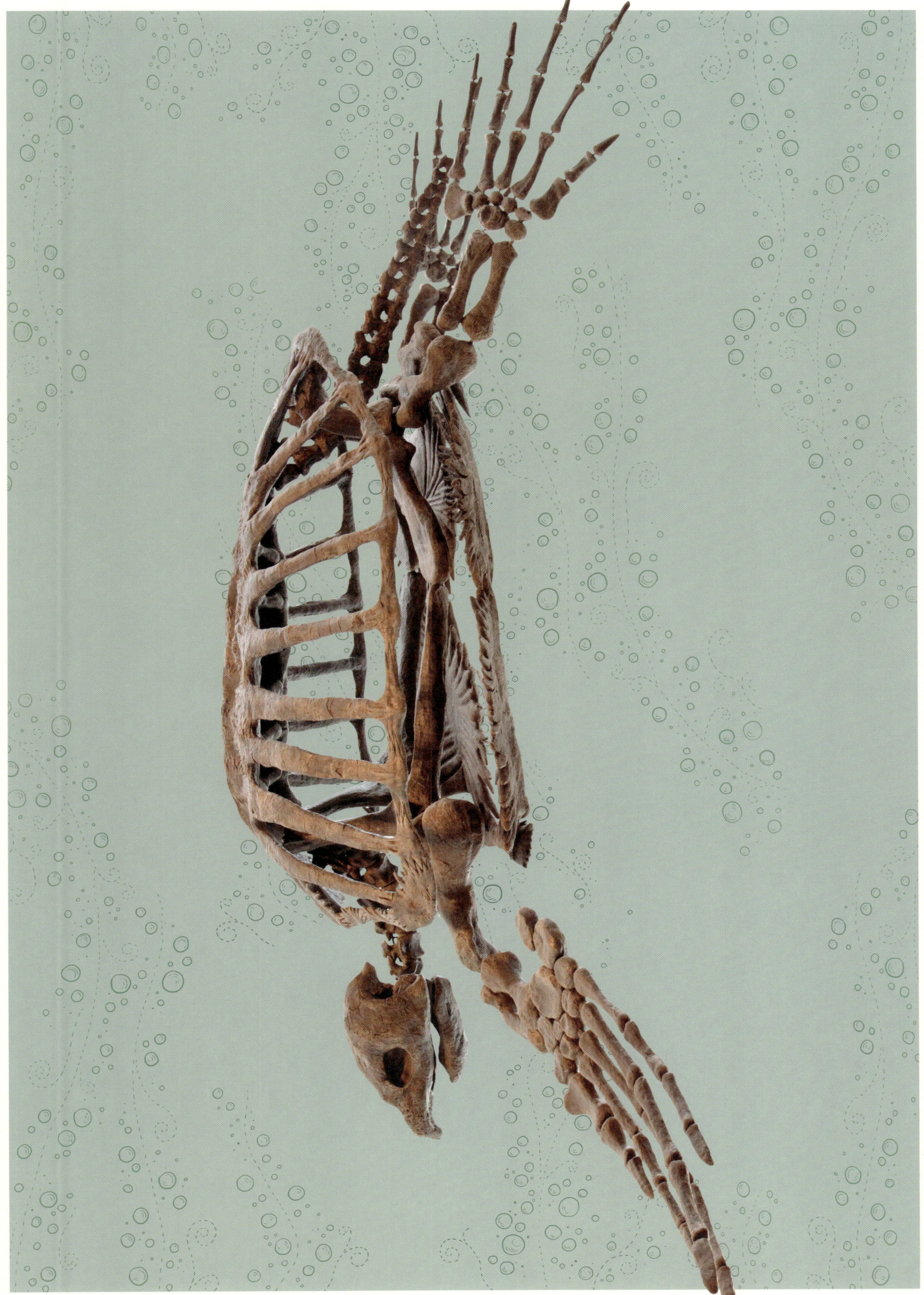

Archelon

Archelon was the largest sea turtle to ever live – it was the size of a car! In order to lay its eggs, it probably had to heave its huge body onto shore, so it could dig a nest in the sand.

Pronunciation: Ar-keh-lon
Period: Cretaceous
Location: North America

Maiasaura

This dinosaur's name means "good mother lizard" because it looked after its young. Each mother carefully built a volcano-shaped nest of mud, in which it laid 30–40 eggs.

Pronunciation: Mai-a-sor-a
Period: Cretaceous
Location: North America

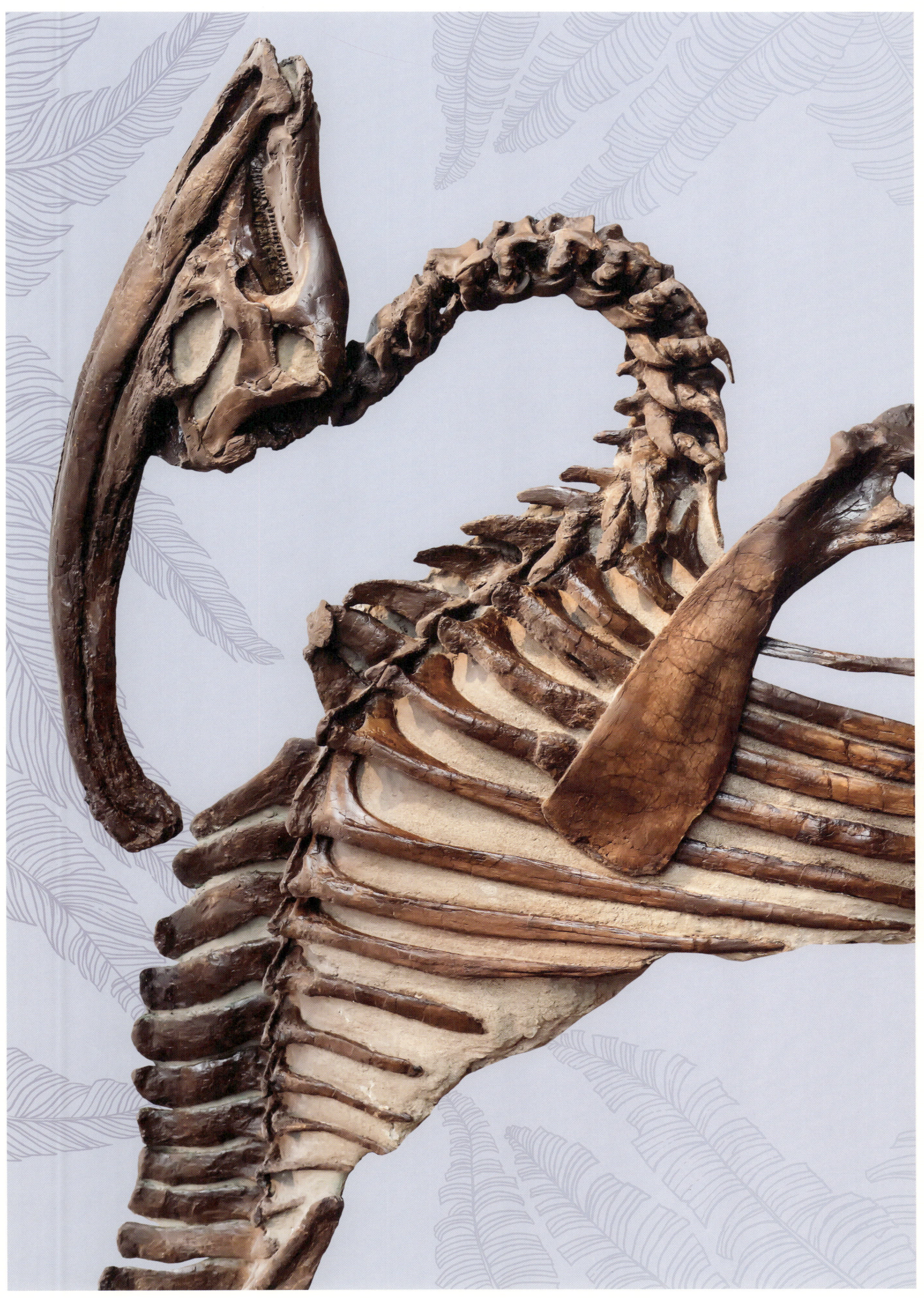

Parasaurolophus

Imagine having a nose as long as three trumpets! Most paleontologists agree that Parasaurolophus used it to make sounds to communicate with other members of its herd.

Pronunciation: Pa-ra-sor-oh-loh-fuss

Period: Cretaceous

Location: North America

Triceratops

Triceratops fossils found with bite marks on suggest they were a regular item on T. rex's menu. However, fossils with healed bones show they sometimes managed to escape!

Pronunciation: Try-seh-ra-tops
Period: Cretaceous
Location: North America

Plioplatecarpus

This was a ferocious mosasaur. Like a snake, its jaws had a double-hinge enabling it to open its mouth sideways as well as up and down, which meant it could swallow most prey whole!

Pronunciation: Ply-oh-plat-ee-karp-uss
Period: Cretaceous
Location: Europe, North America

Velociraptor

About the size of a large dog, this may not have been the largest predator, but it was equipped with up to 60 serrated teeth and a razor-sharp "killer claw" on each foot.

Pronunciation: Veh-loss-i-rap-tuh

Period: Cretaceous

Location: Asia

Styracosaurus

Styracosaurus boasted one of the most elaborate neck frills of any dinosaur. It also had an enormous nose horn, which could grow to 60 cm (24 in) long.

Pronunciation: Sty-ra-koh-sor-uss
Period: Cretaceous
Location: North America

Tyrannosaurus

This is probably the most famous dinosaur. It was among the biggest predators to ever live, and it could eat the equivalent of 4,000 sausages in one bite!

Pronunciation: Tai-ran-oh-sor-uss
Period: Cretaceous
Location: North America

Amber

Amber is the fossilized remains of resin that oozes out of pine trees. Small creatures occasionally get stuck, and it perfectly preserves them — like a time capsule!

Period: Paleogene
Location: Europe

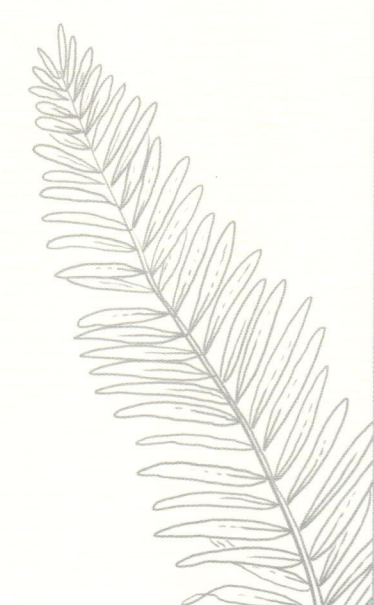

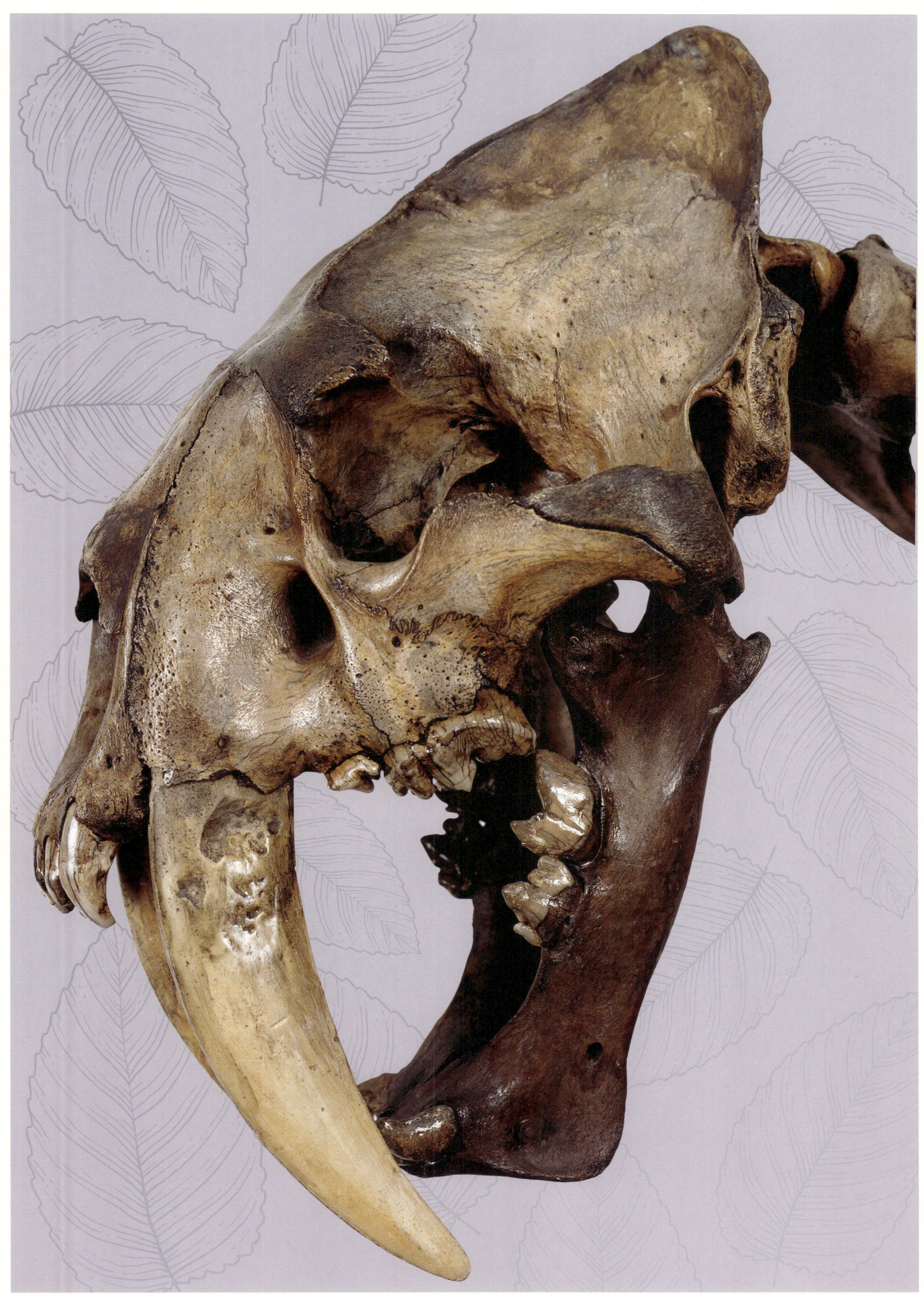

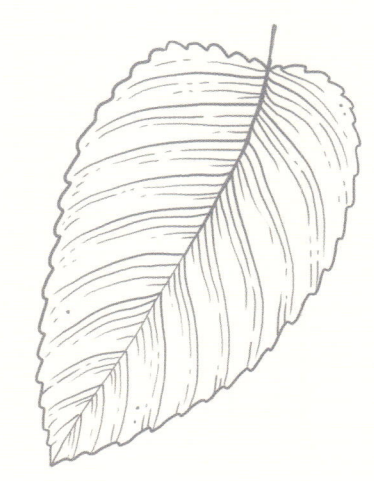

Smilodon

Also known as a sabre-toothed cat because of its sword-like teeth, Smilodon's jaws could open twice as wide as a modern lion to deliver a deadly bite!

Pronunciation: Smy-loh-don
Period: Neogene to Quaternary
Location: North America, South America

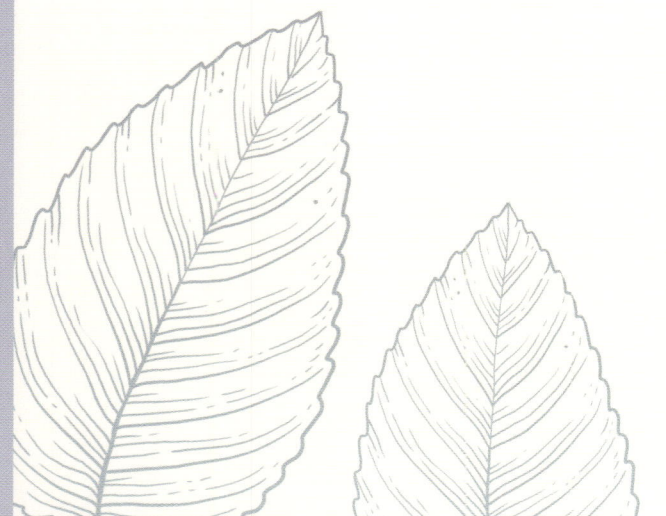
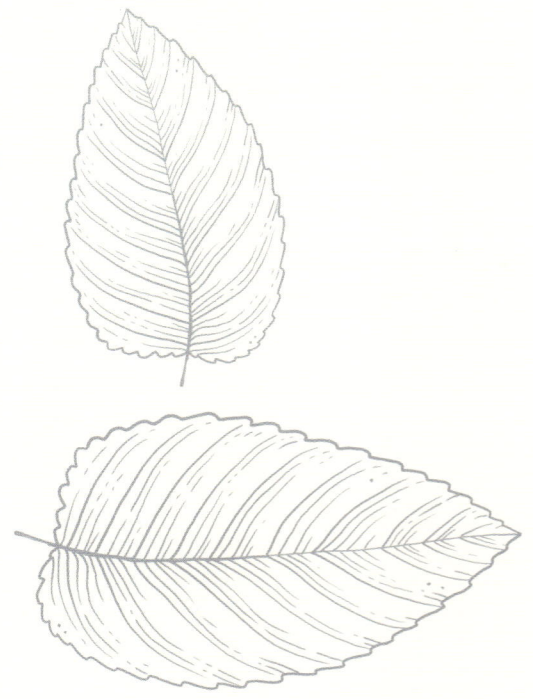

Woolly mammoth

Some woolly mammoths have been discovered perfectly preserved in ice. Most mammoths became extinct at the end of the Ice Age, 10,500 years ago, mainly due to hunting by humans.

Period: Quaternary

Location: Asia, Europe, North America

Dire wolf

Aenocyon dirus, commonly known as the dire wolf, became extinct 10,000 years ago. Their fossils are often found close together, which suggests they lived and hunted in packs.

Pronunciation of scientific name: Ee-noh-sai-on dai-russ

Period: Quaternary

Location: North America, South America

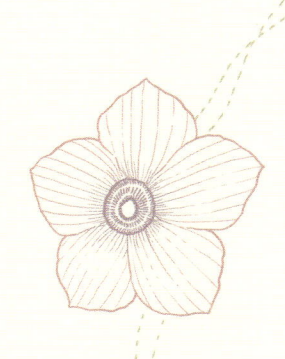

Florissantia

Florissantia is related to the plant from which we make chocolate. No fossils of the leaves have been found, so no one knows what the whole plant looked like.

Pronunciation: Flo-ri-san-tee-a
Period: Paleogene
Location: North America

Megalodon

The scientific name for megalodons is Otodus, which means "ear-shaped tooth". They were the largest sharks that have ever lived, and they had 276 huge teeth!

Pronunciation of scientific name: Oh-toh-duss
Period: Neogene
Location: Worldwide